T0041132

BERKLEE
INSTANT
DRUM SET

RON SAVAGE

Edited by
JONATHAN FEIST

Berklee Media

Associate Vice President: Dave Kusek
Director of Content: Debbie Cavalier
Marketing Manager: Ami Bennitt
Business Manager: Jennifer Rassler

Berklee Press

Senior Writer/Editor: Jonathan Feist
Writer/Editor: Susan Gedutis
Production Manager: Shawn Girsberger

ISBN 978-0-634-02602-7

berklee
press

1140 Boylston Street
Boston, MA 02215-3693 USA
(617) 747-2146

Visit Berklee Press Online at
www.berkleepress.com

DISTRIBUTED BY

HAL•LEONARD®
CORPORATION
7777 W. BLUEMOUND RD. P.O. BOX 13819
MILWAUKEE, WISCONSIN 53213

Visit Hal Leonard Online at
www.halleonard.com

To my wife, Lolita, and my son, Xavier.

Contents

CD Tracks

The Band

Kevin Barry, *Guitars*
Consuelo Candelaria-Barry, *Keyboards*

Tim Ingles, *Bass*
Ron Savage, *Drums*

Lesson 1. The Basic Stroke

CD 01. "Fulcrum Rock"
CD 02. "Fulcrum Rock" (No Drums)

Lesson 2. Keeping Time

CD 03. Whole Notes
CD 04. "Whole Note Rock"
CD 05. "Whole Note Rock" (No Drums)
CD 06. Half Notes
CD 07. "Half Note Rock"
CD 08. "Half Note Rock" (No Drums)
CD 09. Quarter Notes
CD 10. "Quarter Note Rock"
CD 11. "Quarter Note Rock" (No Drums)

Lesson 3. Playing a Beat

CD 12. Making the Beat, "On the One"
CD 13. "On the One"
CD 14. "On the One" (No Drums)
CD 15. "One Up"
CD 16. "One Up" (No Drums)

Lesson 4. Rock

CD 17. Eighth Notes
CD 18. "Rockin' 8"
CD 19. "Rockin' 8" (No Drums)
CD 20. Making the Beat, "Rock Out"
CD 21. "Rock Out"
CD 22. "Rock Out" (No Drums)
CD 23. Making the Beat, "Party Rock"
CD 24. "Party Rock"
CD 25. "Party Rock" (No Drums)

Lesson 5. Fills

CD 26. Beat with Fill
CD 27. Sixteenth-Note Fill
CD 28. Another Sixteenth-Note Fill

CD 29. "Thunder"
CD 30. "Thunder" (No Drums)
CD 31. "Thunder Rock"
CD 32. "Thunder Rock" (No Drums)

Lesson 6. Hi-Hat Variations

CD 33. Hi-Hat
CD 34. Making the Beat, "In the House"
CD 35. "In the House"
CD 36. "In the House" (No Drums)
CD 37. "In the House" with Fill
CD 38. "In the House" with Fill (No Drums)

Lesson 7. Funk

CD 39. Syncopation
CD 40. Making the Beat, "JB's Thing"
CD 41. "JB's Thing"
CD 42. "JB's Thing" (No Drums)
CD 43. "Jabo"
CD 44. "Jabo" (No Drums)

Lesson 8. Swing

CD 45. Swing Feel
CD 46. Hi-Hat Foot
CD 47. Making the Beat, "Swingin' the Blues"
CD 48. "Swingin' the Blues"
CD 49. "Swingin' the Blues" (No Drums)
CD 50. Swing Fills
CD 51. "Slow Down Blues"
CD 52. "Slow Down Blues" (No Drums)

Lesson 9. 12-Bar Blues

CD 53. "L's Blues"
CD 54. "L's Blues" (No Drums)

Welcome to Instant Drum Set

This book will get you playing the drum set instantly. Some friends and I put together a band, and we recorded some really fun music for you to jam with us. The *Instant Drum Set CD* has songs ready for you to play along with *right now!*

For each tune, first check out the CD tracks marked "Listen," which include a drummer. Then, once you've learned the drum part, it's your turn. You'll play along with the tracks marked "Play Along," which have no drums.

So, set up your set, and let's play some music!

Get Ready to Play

The Drum Set

In this book, you'll use a simple drum set with just bass drum, snare drum, ride cymbal, and hi-hat. These are enough to learn the basic skills and to play most styles of music. The techniques are the same for most other drums or cymbals that you will have in your set, such as the crash cymbal, tom-toms, and others. (See the Appendix, "Instrument Index," to learn more about drums and how to tune them.)

Setting Up

Set up your drums so that they are right for you. Set the height and distance of each drum or cymbal so that you can play it without lunging or twisting. Set the *throne* (stool) height so that your feet are flat on the floor, your legs are comfortable, and your back is straight.

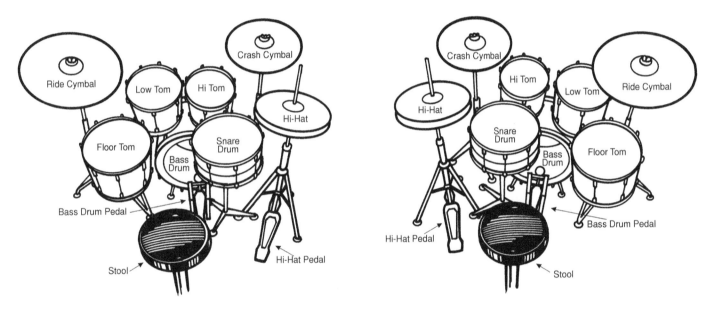

Left-Handed Setup   *Right-Handed Setup*

Playing Position

Sit with your back straight and your arms straight and relaxed, hanging naturally, and pointing towards the floor. Then raise them to a 90-degree angle, staying as relaxed as possible. Keep your back straight. This is your natural playing position. It should be your guide for setting up your drum set and for playing comfortably.

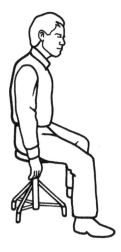 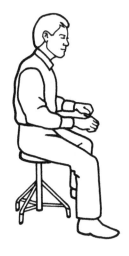

Practice Tips

When you use this book:

1. *Listen first.*

2. *Count out loud while you learn each beat.*

3. *Try to match your beat to the beat on the recording.*

The Basic Stroke

Holding Drumsticks

Hold your sticks between your thumbs and index fingers about a third up from the butt end. This point is called the *fulcrum,* and it is your main point for controlling the stick. Rest your other fingers loosely on the stick without applying any pressure.

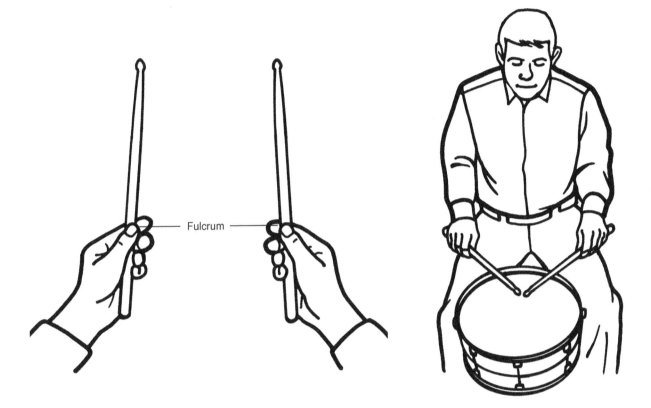

Fulcrum

Get ready to play the snare drum!

1. Hold your right arm at a 90-degree angle.

2. Raise your arm a bit and then snap your wrist down to strike. The tip should hit the middle of the drum head. Let the stick *rebound* (bounce) back to its starting point. Practice this until you can do it comfortably.

3. Slowly, do the same thing with your left hand.

4. When you can play the basic stroke with either hand, practice changing hands every stroke. This is called *alternate sticking*. Play at the center of the drum head. If you find yourself stretching or turning, change the drum's or cymbal's height or move it closer to you.

You've been playing using the *matched grip*—the most common way to hold the sticks. The sticks are gripped the same way in both hands. Now, let's play!

"Fulcrum Rock"

 1. Listen

If you can hold a stick, you can play this tune. Listen to the drum set on the CD. All you hear is the snare drum.

2. Play

Now, play the snare drum on "Fulcrum Rock" along with the band on the CD. Change hands on every stroke, and follow your ear. Play loud or soft—just pick up your sticks and ROCK!

> Play along with the same track, but this time, change hands every stroke: R (right hand), L (left hand), R, L (keep going!).
>
> - Then every two strokes: R R L L R R L L R R L L R R L L...
> - Then every four strokes: R R R R L L L L R R R R L L L L...
> - Then every eight strokes: R R R R R R R R L L L L L L L L...

FULCRUM ROCK

ROCK

[: PLAY THE SNARE DRUM WHENEVER YOU WANT. FOLLOW YOUR EAR. :]

Having a good grip is the most fundamental and vital part of being a good drummer.

Keeping Time

Whole Notes

This is a *whole note* (**o**). It lasts four *beats* (counts). Count a steady 1-2-3-4 whenever you play a whole note.

o

1   2   3   4

Listen to the bass guitar on the recording. It plays four counts while the snare plays each whole note. The snare drum plays with the bass guitar on beat 1 of every bar. Hit the snare drum when you say "1," and count "2, 3, 4" while you wait to come in again. Vertical lines called *bar lines* (|) separate each group (*bar* or *measure*) of four beats.

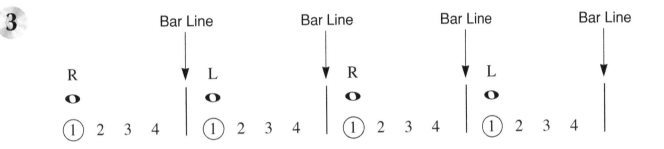

> **Tip:** Play at exactly the same time as the bass guitar on beat 1. This is called **hooking up**.

Bass and drums play the music's foundation.

"Whole Note Rock"

4 1. Listen

This tune is like "Fulcrum Rock," but the drums play steady whole notes on the snare.

5 2. Play

Play along with "Whole Note Rock." Hook up with bass guitar on beat 1 of every bar.

WHOLE NOTE ROCK

ROCK

o		o		o		o	
1 2 3 4		1 2 3 4		1 2 3 4		1 2 3 4	

Half Notes

In this next tune, the drums play *half notes*. Half notes ($\half$) get two beats.

*   Play on 1, count on 2, play on 3, count on 4.

*   Use alternate sticking.

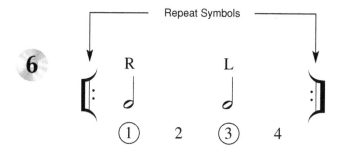

6

Tip: *When you see the* **repeat symbols** [: :] *, play that part again before continuing on.*

"Half Note Rock"

7 ## 1. Listen

This drum part is like the one in "Whole Rock," but with half notes on the snare.

8 ## 2. Play

Hook up with the bass guitar on beats 1 and 3.

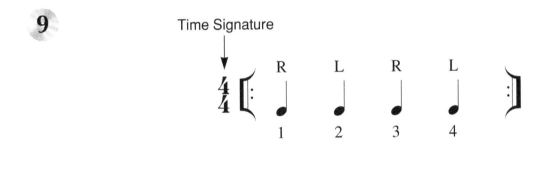

Quarter Notes

In this next tune, the drums play *quarter notes*. Quarter notes (♩) get one beat, so you'll play on every count. Throughout this lesson, the bass guitar has always been playing quarter notes.

9

> *Tip:* In a **time signature** (*4/4*), the top number tells you how many beats are in each measure. The bottom number tells you the note value of each beat. In this book, all time signatures are 4/4, meaning that there are four beats in each measure and each beat lasts for a quarter (1/4) note.

"Quarter Note Rock"

10 1. Listen

Listen to the quarter-note pulse. Quarter notes are the basic unit of most drum-set music.

11 2. Play

Play quarter notes on the snare drum (R L R L). Try playing quarter notes on the snare drum, bass drum, and hi-hat. Hook up with the bass guitar on every beat.

A drummer's first job is always to play good, steady time.

Playing a Beat

A *drum beat* is a set of rhythms usually played on several drums or cymbals in your kit. A *staff* shows what instruments you should play. Each line or space is used for a different drum or cymbal.

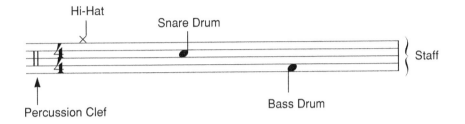

Tip: *X noteheads (♩) mean cymbals, and solid dot noteheads (♩) mean drums.*
X noteheads on the space above the staff are played on the hi-hat.

Making the Beat

12 For each step, first listen to the recorded beat. Practice that step by yourself until you can play it comfortably. Then practice it along with the recording.

Start with the Hi-Hat

When you learn a new drum beat, always start with the hi-hat. Play this quarter-note hi-hat groove along with the CD. Keep your foot down on the hi-hat pedal. Use just enough foot pressure to keep the cymbals from clanging or buzzing.

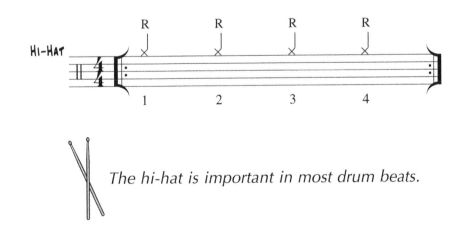

The hi-hat is important in most drum beats.

Add the Bass Drum

When you play bass drum, keep your leg relaxed, your toes straight, and your heel down on the ground. Work the pedal with the ball of your foot.

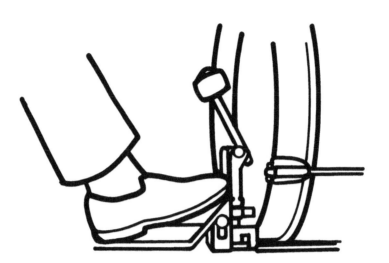

While you play your hi-hat quarter notes, add the bass drum on counts 1 and 3. The bass drum part is written on the lowest space on the staff. Rests (𝄽) mean "don't play."

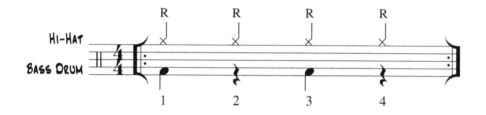

Add the Snare Drum

The snare drum part will complete your beat. Play the hi-hat and bass drum parts, and then add the snare drum on beats 2 and 4. This completes the "basic groove."

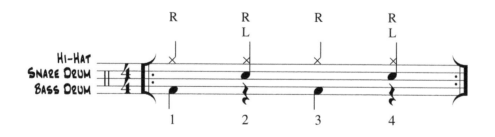

Tip: Note stems pointing up are for drums or cymbals played with your hands.
Note stems pointing down are for drums or cymbals played with your feet.

"On the One"

13 **1. Listen**

This tune uses the beat you just learned.

14 **2. Play**

Count while you play.

ON THE ONE

"One Up"

15 **1. Listen**

This tune uses the same beat, just faster.

16 **2. Play**

Count while you play.

ONE UP

Eighth Notes

Rock drum beats often have a busier feel than the beats you have been playing. In the next beat you learn, instead of just one note for each count, you will play two notes for each count, "1 + 2 + 3 + 4 +" (say "and" for "+"). These rhythms are called *eighth notes*. Groups of eighth notes are connected by a beam (♩♩). Single eighth notes have flags (♪).

17 Practice eighth notes on the snare drum. Change hands on every stroke (R L R L...).

Practice eighth notes on the hi-hat. Use just your right hand for every stroke (R R R R...).

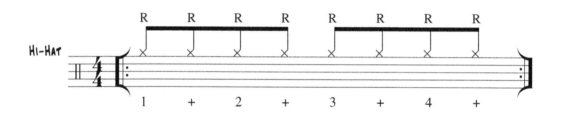

"Rockin' 8"

18 ## 1. Listen

Count while you listen to this eighth-note groove.

19 ## 2. Play

Count while you play.

ROCKIN' 8

Making the Beat

Now let's play a drum beat with an eighth-note feel.

20 For each step, listen, practice, and then play along with the recording.

- Start with the hi-hat.

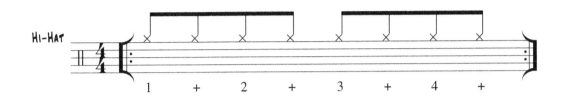

- Add the bass drum.

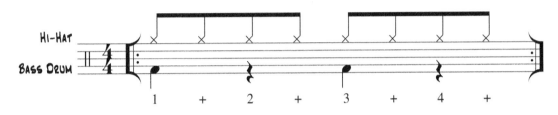

- Add the snare drum.

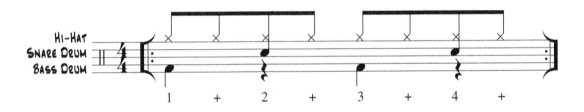

> *Tip:* You can vary the hi-hat's sound by using the pedal. Release the pressure a bit so that the cymbals are slightly separated—just a fraction of an inch. This lets them ring out slightly and gives them a bigger sound.

"Rock Out"

21 **1. Listen**

Count while you listen to this eighth-note groove.

22 **2. Play**

Count out loud while you play.

ROCK OUT

23 **Making the Beat**

This next rock groove is similar to "Rock Out," but the bass drum is different.

For each step, listen, practice, and then play along with the recording.

• Start with the hi-hat.

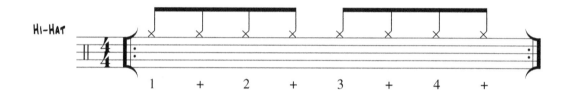

• Add the new bass drum part. Make sure that the bass drum notes are together with the hi-hat.

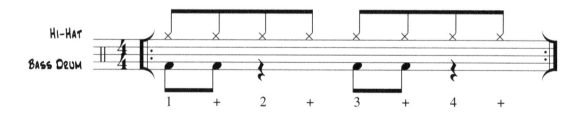

• Add the snare drum on beats 2 and 4.

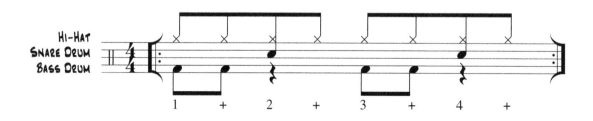

12

"Party Rock"

24 1. Listen

Count while you listen to this eighth-note groove.

25 2. Play

Count out loud while you play.

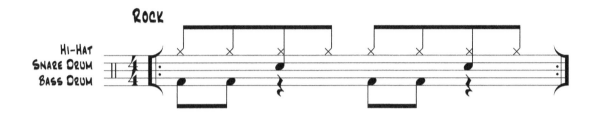

Lesson Five **Fills**

Fills are variations in the beat, often played on the snare drum or tom-toms. They may signal to the other musicians that a change is coming in the music. Usually, fills occur at the end of a phrase—every four or eight measures. They can be very short. Many fills last only a beat or two.

26 Listen to the beat on the recording. Notice where the fill is located. The recorded fill lasts for two beats, and it is played on the snare drum. It comes at the end of each 4-bar phrase.

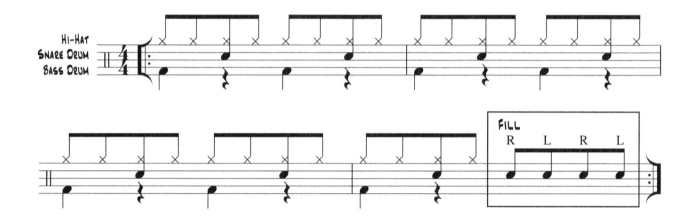

Sixteenth-Note Fills

Some fills use *sixteenth-note* rhythms. Sixteenth notes are twice as fast as eighth notes. They have two beams (𝅘𝅥𝅯) or two flags (𝅘𝅥𝅯). There are four sixteenth notes per beat, or sixteen for each 4/4 measure.

27 Count "1 e + a, 2 e + a, 3 e + a, 4 e + a" (say "ee and uh") as you practice this sixteenth-note fill on your snare drum. This fill could also end a phrase.

28 Here is another fill that uses sixteenth notes.

"Thunder"

29 1. Listen

Count the measures as you listen. The fill comes at the end of every eight bars.

30 2. Play

The "6 Bars Groove" means to continue the beat for six more bars. You'll play the beat for a total of seven bars and then play the fill.

"Thunder Rock"

31 1. Listen

Listen for the flow of the eighth notes connecting the hi-hat and bass drum.

32 2. Play

Notice that this fill is a combination of eighth notes and sixteenth notes. Make sure the transition between them is smooth.

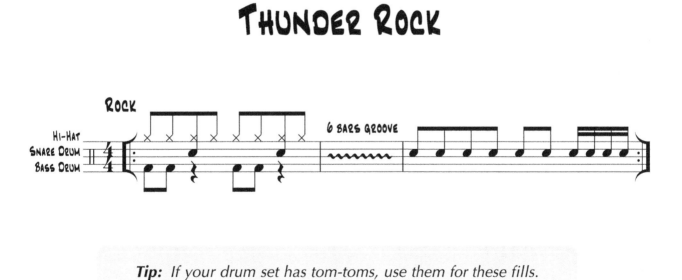

Tip: *If your drum set has tom-toms, use them for these fills.*

33 1. Listen

The hi-hat can be played open or closed. A circle (○) above the note means "play it open" by pressing the foot pedal to separate the cymbals. Listen to the recording. Then practice this hi-hat line until you can play it easily.

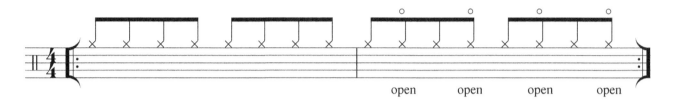

Making the Beat

34 For each step, listen, practice, and then play along with the recording.

- Start with the hi-hat. Be sure to open and close the hi-hat smoothly.

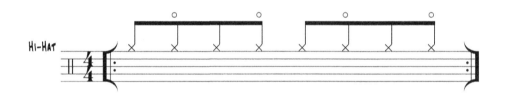

- Add the bass drum. Both feet should go up and down at the same time on the bass drum and the hi-hat. Keep the bass drum steady on all four beats.

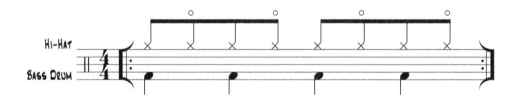

- Add the snare drum. Play the snare drum on beats 2 and 4.

"In the House"

1. Listen

Listen closely to the sound of the hi-hat.

2. Play

When you play, try to open and close the hi-hat evenly.

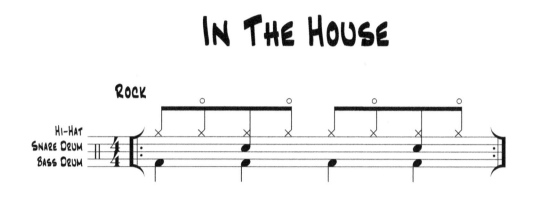

IN THE HOUSE

> **Tip:** Count along with the beat, "1-2-3-4." This will help you hook up with the rest of the band, and get you inside the song's rhythm.

"In the House" (with Fill)

37 1. Listen

This tune uses the fill you learned in the previous lesson.

38 2. Play

Play the fill clearly and evenly.

IN THE HOUSE (WITH FILL)

Syncopated notes are played off the beat—when you say "and," not when you say a number. Here is a bass drum part where there is a syncopation on the "and" of beat 3. At beat 3, there is an *eighth-note rest* ( ), which lasts for half a beat.

39 Listen

Listen to the recorded beat, and then try to play along with this bass drum part.

Making the Beat

40 For each step, listen, practice, and then play along with the recording.

• Start with the hi-hat.

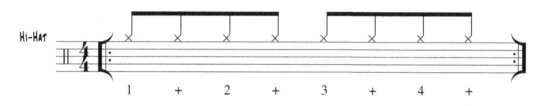

• Add the syncopated bass drum part you have been practicing. It has a syncopation off beat 3.

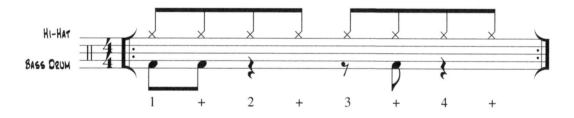

• Add the snare drum part. It has a syncopation off beat 2. The snare also plays right on beat 4.

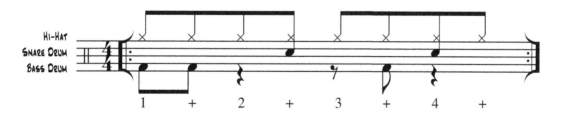

"J.B.'s Thing"

1. Listen

Listen to how the bass drum and bass guitar sound together.

2. Play

When playing syncopated eighth notes, be sure to keep the tempo steady.

J.B.'S THING

Tip: Practice any new beat at different tempos (speeds). First, practice it very slowly. Then gradually, speed it up until it is as fast as you can play it without making any mistakes.

"Jabo"

43 ## 1. Listen

This tune has the same beat, but it is at a faster tempo. The bass and drums keep the groove locked in.

44 ## 2. Play

When you play at faster tempos, be sure your body is relaxed.

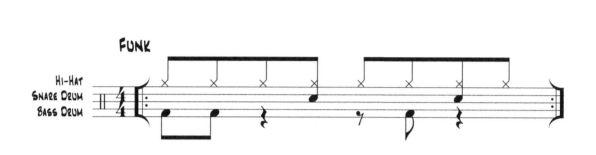

Lesson Eight Swing

45 Swing Feel

Listen to the ride cymbal playing a jazz pattern. The eighth notes are played with a *swing feel*. All notes should have an even, relaxed sound.

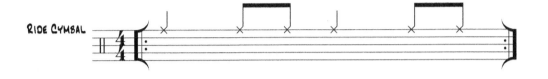

> *Tip:* The ride cymbal part is an X-notehead on the top line.

Hi-Hat Foot

46 Another way to jazz up your beat is to add the hi-hat foot, played using the foot pedal. In jazz, this sound is often used on beats 2 and 4.

> *Tip:* The hi-hat foot part is an X-notehead on the bottom line. Whenever you see the stem pointing down (hi-hat foot or bass drum), you play that part with your feet.

47 Making the Beat

For each step, listen, practice, and then play along with the recording.

- Start with the ride cymbal playing the jazz pattern. Play the eighth notes with a swing feel.

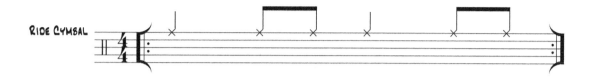

- Add the bass drum. Keep the quarter notes smooth and even.

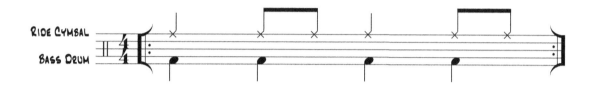

- Add the hi-hat foot. Play nice and easy on beats 2 and 4.

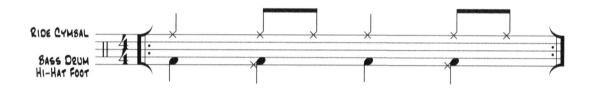

"Swingin' the Blues"

48 1. Listen

Listen to the ride cymbal swinging the eighth notes.

49 2. Play

Make the bass drum smooth and soft.

SWINGIN' THE BLUES

Swing Fills

 Try this fill in your swing tunes.

Tip: When you see slash marks (╱ ╱ ╱ ╱), it means "create your own part." Play anything you want, as long as it fits the tune. The word "fill" means you should stop playing the regular beat and create your own fill.

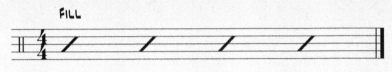

"Slow Down Blues"

51 ## 1. Listen

This tune uses the same beat, but faster. Listen to the sound and rhythm of the hi-hat. It is the same jazz pattern that you heard on the ride cymbal.

52 ## 2. Play

When you play the hi-hat part, use the same rhythm and phrasing as you played on the ride cymbal. At the fill, play the fill you learned in this lesson or your own fill.

> **Tip:** Learn any new beat by adding one drum or cymbal at a time. Start with hi-hat (or ride cymbal), then add bass drum, and then snare drum.

12-Bar Blues

53 Listen

As you listen, count the measures. Listen for the chord progression in the rest of the band. Notice that every twelve measures, it repeats. That's what makes this tune a *12-bar blues*. Its *form* (repeating shape) is twelve measures long, and the chords (played by the rest of the band) change according to the pattern below. The drums signal the end of the form with a fill.

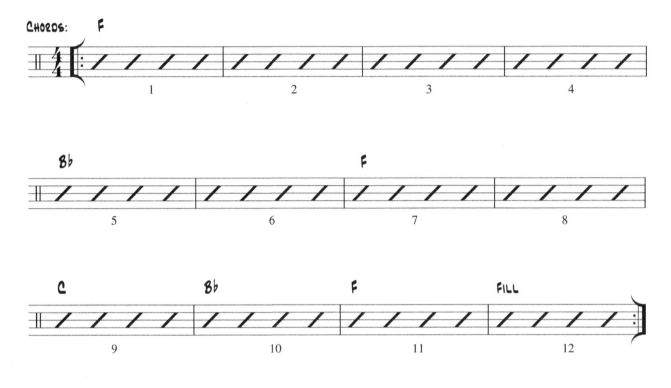

"L's Blues"

53 1. Listen

Listen to how the hi-hat is used during the melody.

54 2. Play

Try playing the ride cymbal and the hi-hat during different parts of the song.

L's Blues

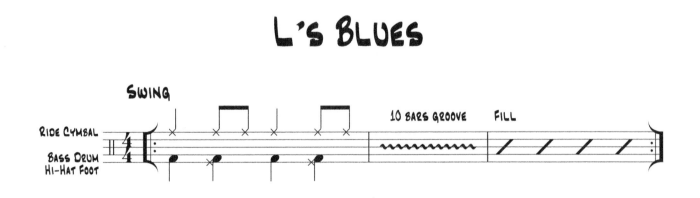

Author's Note

Thanks for playing *Instant Drum Set*. You now have the skills to begin playing a wide variety of songs. Always remember to listen, pay attention to the music, and enjoy playing with other musicians. Good luck, and keep swingin'!

—Ron Savage

Appendix. Instrument Index

The drums and cymbals in a drum set come in a wide variety of sounds. Generally, the louder and more aggressive the music, the bigger the drums and the heavier the cymbals. When you are buying your first drum set, ask an experienced drummer to help you choose the right instrument for the music you want to play.

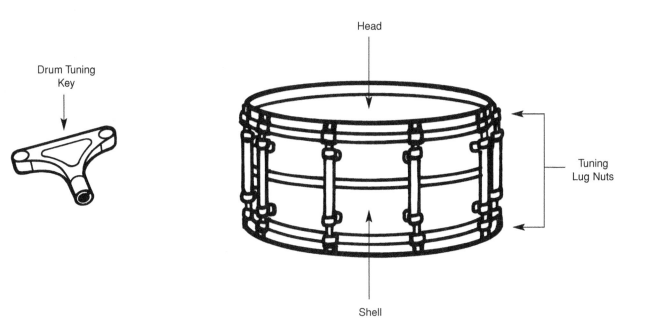

Head

Drum Tuning Key

Tuning Lug Nuts

Shell

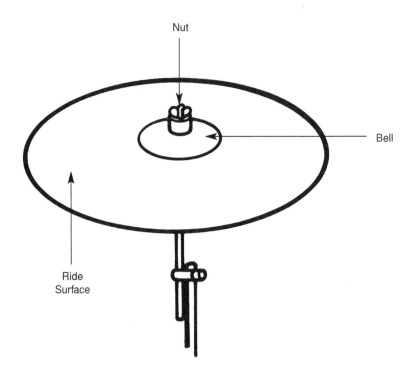

Nut

Bell

Ride Surface

Tuning

Tuning your drums brings out their best sound. To tune your drums, adjust the tension of the heads by turning the lug nuts with your drum tuning key. First tune the top head (playing head) to the best sound that you can get. Then tune the bottom head to the same sound. Tune your drums every time you play.

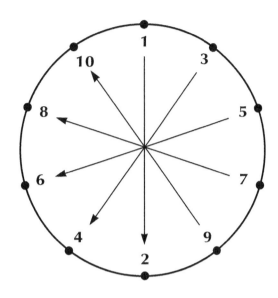

1. With the tuning key, tighten the tuning lugs only slightly, until they just begin to resist turning.

2. Tighten the lugs in the numerical order shown in the chart above. Keep tapping the head near the center to test the sound. When you reach the sound you want, move on to the next lug.

3. Repeat this process on the bottom head.

Different drums are tuned to different sounds. Here is a guide to the drums you are likely to have in your set.

The **snare drum** has snares (wires) on the bottom that you can raise and lower to give different sounds. Drum sizes range from 12 to 14 inches in diameter and from 4 to 6 inches in depth. Tune it to have a crisp sound, with the snares just tight enough to buzz smoothly. Snare drums are also common in marching bands and orchestras. They are played as a regular part of the beat.

The **bass drum** is played with a foot pedal. Drum sizes range from 16 to 24 inches in diameter and from 14 to 18 in depth. Tune it to have a heavy, deep, resonant tone. A pillow inside it will give a heavier thump. Bass drums are also common in marching bands and orchestras. They are played as a regular part of the beat.

Hi-hat cymbals are two cymbals that can be pressed together. They are played with a foot pedal and with sticks at the same time. Sizes range from 12 to 15 inches in diameter. They are played as a regular part of the beat.

Ride and crash cymbals are played with sticks. Crashes generally range from 10 to 20 inches in diameter. Ride cymbals are usually heavier than crash cymbals and range in size from 18 to 22 inches in diameter. They are often used as a regular part of the beat ("riding") or for accents.

Tom-toms, including mounted toms and floor toms, are played with sticks. They are also usually tuned so that each tom has a different sound. Sizes range from 6 to 18 inches in diameter and depth. They are mainly used for fills and accents.

TOOLS FOR DJs

**TURNTABLE TECHNIQUE:
THE ART OF THE DJ**
▸ by Stephen Webber
50449482 Book/2-Record Set $34.95

TURNTABLE BASICS ▸ by Stephen Webber
50449514 Book $9.95

VITAL VINYL, VOLUMES 1-5
▸ by Stephen Webber
12" records
50449491 Volume 1: Needle Juice $15.95
50449492 Volume 2: Turntablist's Toolkit.......$15.95
50449493 Volume 3: Rockin' the House $15.95
50449494 Volume 4: Beat Bomb $15.95
50449495 Volume 5: Tech Tools for DJs $15.95

TOOLS FOR DJs SUPERPACK
▸ by Stephen Webber
50449529 Includes Turntable Technique book/2-record
set and all 5 Vital Vinyl records (a $115 value!) ..$99.95

BERKLEE PRACTICE METHOD

Get Your Band Together

BASS ▸ by Rich Appleman and John Repucci
50449427 Book/CD....................................$14.95

DRUM SET ▸ by Ron Savage and
Casey Scheuerell
50449429 Book/CD....................................$14.95

GUITAR ▸ by Larry Baione
50449426 Book/CD....................................$14.95

KEYBOARD ▸ by Russell Hoffmann and
Paul Schmeling
50449428 Book/CD....................................$14.95

ALTO SAX ▸ by Jim Odgren and Bill Pierce
50449437 Book/CD....................................$14.95

TENOR SAX ▸ by Jim Odgren and Bill Pierce
50449431 Book/CD....................................$14.95

TROMBONE ▸ by Jeff Galindo
50449433 Book/CD....................................$14.95

TRUMPET ▸ by Tiger Okoshi and Charles
Lewis
50449432 Book/CD....................................$14.95

INSTANT SERIES

BASS ▸ by Danny Morris
50449502 Book/CD....................................$14.95

DRUM SET ▸ by Ron Savage
50449513 Book/CD....................................$14.95

GUITAR ▸ by Tomo Fujita
50449522 Book/CD....................................$14.95

KEYBOARD ▸ by Paul Schmeling and
Dave Limina
50449525 Book/CD....................................$14.95

IMPROVISATION SERIES

BLUES IMPROVISATION COMPLETE ▸
by Jeff Harrington ▸ Book/CD Packs
50449486 Bb Instruments $19.95
50449488 C Bass Instruments $19.95
50449425 C Treble Instruments $19.95
50449487 Eb Instruments $19.95

A GUIDE TO JAZZ IMPROVISATION
▸ by John LaPorta ▸ Book/CD Packs
50449439 C Instruments $16.95
50449441 Bb Instruments $16.95
50449442 Eb Instruments $16.95
50449443 Bass Clef $16.95

MUSIC TECHNOLOGY

ARRANGING IN THE DIGITAL WORLD
▸ by Corey Allen
50449415 Book/GM disk $19.95

**FINALE: AN EASY GUIDE TO MUSIC
NOTATION** ▸ by Thomas E. Rudolph and
Vincent A. Leonard, Jr.
50449501 Book/CD-ROM $59.95

**PRODUCING IN THE HOME STUDIO
WITH PRO TOOLS** ▸ by David Franz
50449526 Book/CD-ROM $34.95

RECORDING IN THE DIGITAL WORLD
▸ by Thomas E. Rudolph and
Vincent A. Leonard, Jr.
50449472 Book $29.95

MUSIC BUSINESS

**HOW TO GET A JOB IN THE MUSIC &
RECORDING INDUSTRY**
▸ by Keith Hatschek
50449505 Book $24.95

THE SELF-PROMOTING MUSICAN
▸ by Peter Spellman
50449423 Book $24.95

THE MUSICIAN'S INTERNET
▸ by Peter Spellman
50449527 Book $24.95

REFERENCE

COMPLETE GUIDE TO FILM SCORING
▸ by Richard Davis
50449417 Book $24.95

THE CONTEMPORARY SINGER
▸ by Anne Peckham
50449438 Book/CD...$24.95

ESSENTIAL EAR TRAINING
▸ by Steve Prosser
50449421 Book $14.95

MODERN JAZZ VOICINGS ▸ by Ted
Pease and Ken Pullig
50449485 Book/CD...$24.95

**THE NEW MUSIC THERAPIST'S
HANDBOOK, SECOND EDITION**
▸ by Suzanne B. Hanser
50449424 Book $29.95

POP CULTURE

INSIDE THE HITS
▸ by Wayne Wadhams
50449476 Book $29.95

**MASTERS OF MUSIC:
CONVERSATIONS WITH
BERKLEE GREATS** ▸ by Mark Small and
Andrew Taylor
50449422 Book $24.95

SONGWRITING

MELODY IN SONGWRITING
▸ by Jack Perricone
50449419 Book $19.95

MUSIC NOTATION ▸ by Mark McGrain
50449399 Book $19.95

**SONGWRITING: ESSENTIAL GUIDE
TO LYRIC FORM AND STRUCTURE**
▸ by Pat Pattison
50481582 Book $14.95

**SONGWRITING: ESSENTIAL GUIDE
TO RHYMING** ▸ by Pat Pattison
50481583 Book $14.95